COUNTING OUT THE MILLENNIUM

by

John Oughton

Pecan Grove Press San Antonio, Texas

Copyright © 1996 by John Oughton

All rights reserved by the author

Cover art by Sharon McMahon
Global Perspecive #1
©1997 by the artist

Back Cover Photo:
"Self-Portrait" by John Oughton

ISBN: 1-877603-37-6

Pecan Grove Press
1 Camino Santa Maria
San Antonio, Texas 78228-8608

For my daughter Erin, who renews me

ACKNOWLEDGEMENTS

The author is grateful to the Ontario Arts Council for its support through the Writers' Reserve Program, and to the various publishers who have recommended grants through this program.

Some of these poems previously appeared in *Rampike, Waves, Prism International, Toronto Life, Chili Verde Review, Birthstone, Poetry Toronto, SHIT Magazine, The Swift Current Anthology* and the chapbook *rimbaud's twisted balls* (2 bit poetry no. 16), *Grasslands Review, The XY Files: poems about the male experience, Tender Is the Net* and on the electronic newsgroups Swift Current, crewrt-l@lists.missouri.edu, and rec.arts.poems.

Special thanks to Patricia Valdata and Libby Zöe Oughton for proofreading the manuscript and making many positive suggestions.

*"I stood on the edge of things, as on a circle inscribed,
But time's revolutions have borne me into the still centre."*

—Hafiz of Shiraz, translated by Peter Avery and John Heath-Stubbs.

Notes on the Poems

    Although the poems in this collection range over many styles and themes, several share a concern with the continuance of literature. They draw energy from writing of the past, and consider whether the written-on-paper word is likely to survive the year 2000.

    After completing my previous book on Mata Hari, I found a new persona seizing my imagination. The character of Dr. Syntax was originated in 1812 by the English artist Thomas Rowlandson and fleshed out in verses by a prolific hack journalist named William Combe (now remembered only for the Doctor Syntax series). Syntax, a thin, perpetually broke preacher and teacher, applies his poetic and artistic talents to turning out a best-seller. He tours England on his faithful horse Grizzle, "in search of the Picturesque," capturing whatever he encounters in verse and line drawings. Several poems in my collection explicitly or implicitly imagine Dr. Syntax's reactions to contemporary culture and Canada. In the poem "Edville," the italicized phrases are quoted from signs on the store's exterior.

    The three "Deliberate Mistranslations of Rimbaud" were improvised by finding the nearest phonetic equivalents in English to the French words, rather than translating the sense of the original prose poems in Rimbaud's *Illuminations*. Thus, they are in no way the responsibility of that adolescent genius. "The Perceivability of Poetry" is in part constructed by similar phonetic twists on three sentences, this time in English, from a Bell Telephone advertisement.

    The other poems frame my own tour of this unpredictable era.

Contents

I. Counting Out the Millennium

Notes from the Travel Journal of Dr. Syntax   15
The Boulder   17
Industrial Arts Dream   18
What's Real at the Mars Cafe   20
Edville   21
California Mummy Dummy   23
Renovating Hell   24
The Child Murderer   25
Parliament St. Tableau   26
The Shuttle   27
Unscheduled Train Stop   29

II. Arrivals & Departures Level

Growing Up a Block Away from John McCrae   33
Half-Baked Moon   34
Xmas Pageant, 1961   35
Painting of "The Immaculate Conception"
    in the Scottish National Gallery   37
Dead Skunk on the Don Valley Parkway   38
Hanged Man   39
Lacuna   40
Leaving the Cape   41
Ode to the TD Bank   42
Appearance in Pier Four   43
Epithalamium for Pam   45
Erin's Birth   46
For Erin   48
Back to You   49

Pam & Nimbus   50
Exorcism   51
Variation on a Theme by Erik Satie   53
I'm in Love with My Hoover   54
Dream Game   55
All That Counts   56
Cat Ending   58
The Man on Our Porch   59
Proposal for Prince Charles   61
Being in/Seeing the Body   63
Open House   65
Stroke/Oblique   67

III. Twisting the Tongue

Canadian Love Song   71
The Perceivability of Poetry   72
The White Page   74
Rimbaud Deliberately Mistranslated (I)   76
Rimbaud Deliberately Mistranslated (II)   77
Rimbaud Deliberately Mistranslated (III)   78
William Tell's Son Speaks   79
Hagar the Halfling   81
The World Screened   82

About John Oughton   84

I. COUNTING OUT THE MILLENNIUM

There was so much handwriting on the wall
That even the wall fell down.
—Christopher Morley

NOTES FROM THE TRAVEL JOURNAL OF DR. SYNTAX

1. Signals
To be mad all that's required
is to stand in one place and
understand all signals passing through your head
radio TV radar microwaves shortwave CB RF
X-band K-band satellite voices data ghosts
cops pilots and lonely hearts
talk shows hot picks newsbits and traffic watches
static all the cellular and stellar babble
that one voice talking alone denies
even this voice

2. Saints
To name the habitations of Quebec
explorers ran through the whole canon of saints
and then some
to avoid yet another St. Marie or Joseph
they revived some forgotten even by the Pope—
St. Zotique
roasted by a lightning bolt while praying
in his penitential iron underwear
St. Télèsphore
poisoned by a mushroom he thought
would allow divines to communicate over a distance
St. Louis du-Ha! Ha!
who finally understood what it all meant
and died laughing
St. Eusèbe
who swore he'd sit on a stalactite for 32 years
and pray
and did so until one day a voice mortified him
by informing him it was a stalagmite.
So many saints protect the landscape here
that they collide overhead
in the fog of prayers for intercession and release

3. National Unity
this nation is a fiction
held together only by stamps and money
that proclaim it exists and confer value
the lobster fisherman in Souris
and the lumberjack in Fort St. John
understand totally different Canadas
from the stockbroker in Montreal
and the professor of advanced studies in
Winnipeg. They use the same name
for different nations
only I know my Canada
but I'll lend it to you in these words

THE BOULDER

Near Rivière-du-Loup
above the sweep of the St. Lawrence
a granite heart
taller than a man
interrupts a seigneural field
otherwise perfectly plowed

Rock has maintained its place since the first settler
switched his ox around it and swore
one day he'd dig that boulder out

but over the years
the St. Lawrence below filling and flowing with the tides
that jog in plowing became part of the dance
the farmer and seasons performed with the land
the earth below his clogs now mud,
then awash in wheat, then frozen
the boulder unchanging:
touchstone, always winter in heart

The farmer's son swore too
first at the boulder
then that it would go
as did his son's son and grandson
each came to respect it
could not afford the void
yanking it would make in his life

the boulder withstood them all
as it now withstands my eyes
I swear this poem will move it
for my lines cut straight
(yet the boulder sits)

INDUSTRIAL ARTS DREAM

The industrial artist chartered a copter
to drop the critics and corporate patrons
at the bottom of the gravel pit
that a bemused absentee-landlord holding company
let him use
for what he said would be *definitive* on
how technology changes landscape.

The audience surveyed the work
as the artist waved from the chopper
now perched on the quarry's rim.
Lava flowed towards their feet:
down one side a torrent of electrical cable,
wrapped in black,
exposed copper filaments like nerves
beside it, some blue chemical declined in slow waves
that popped at the crests in iridescent bubbles

and across the pit, constructing a balancing diagonal mass,
a surf of white foam descended.
The quarry's side could be seen only
between a mobile of PCB-daubed transformer parts
and the trellis of used bridge struts dipped in crude oil.
How pleasing to note the umber simplicity of earth
not only as a reminder of the ground
against which all art figures,
but also for its suggestion of an avenue of escape.

As one the pundits and patrons moved towards the path,
masking their worry in discourse of earthworks, trash art,
driving a stake through the heart of modernism.
Above them some diesel machine

uttered a ribbon of glowing slag
to cover the last stripe of earth
and complete the installation.

Baffled, the audience stood and turned,
art at last bigger than they were,
yet somehow they completed it,
their tiny cries adding that note of angst
that kept the piece from descending to one more gloss
on the well-worn theme of our rape of the earth.

WHAT'S REAL AT THE MARS CAFE

The Mars Cafe boasts
"Food That Is Out Of This World"
I sample the conversation
of three business suits in the next booth
who expand upon
start-up capital, Florida developments, mixed-use concepts
my mind drifts to muffin as metaphor
when one says:
"You see, it's really just the words that count.
You say 'pre-fab,' and buyers turn right off.
They don't like the sound of it.
But you just gotta call it something else
like 'sandwich wall construction.' "
His colleague added, "Or podgurney!"
"Sure, podgurney. And then they'll buy it.
It's all in the words."

Confirming again for me
that language is the only real
estate we build on.
These men deal not in earth
ripe with worms and dead leaves
nor in constructions
nailed together,
but in their own peculiar words
that fence off their estate
of the real

EDVILLE
(I live two blocks away from Honest Ed's, the self-proclaimed "world's biggest discount store.")

Circus lights shout Honest Ed
over and over, three stories high
and two blocks long, a legend built of tiny bulbs
that burn all night in bi-bi-binary code.
Ed, in his honesty, owns
the block and more. He bought it by selling
for less more than anyone else. And he never
sold out to modesty. Every word ever written
about him is displayed in the windows to prove it.
The world turns to Ed
to see just how cheap a man can be
turns into Ed, or fails.

Take the Edsel. Ford should have asked Ed
before launching it. He would have made the car
a hit, his face set into the grille's
halo of chrome. Take the moon.
The Yanks got there without Idea One
what to do with it. Ed, in his space suit
and tie, writ large with funny sayings and
bargain boasts, would have zoned it for Sunday openings
and sold the dark side to insomniacs,
the craters to park flying saucers,
the moondust to scour the pots of the poor
always willing to line up
for a deal from Ed. Because
there's no place like this place anyplace.

Now the shadow of the CN Tower
points like an hour hand
from Ed's restaurants to his store
and a flotilla of security guards, chestnut sellers

and buyers of busts of the Pope
sets out in the rolling wake
of his Edship
the Lord Mayor of Edville
the megaphone of himself

CALIFORNIA MUMMY DUMMY
(from a news item)

Your tumbleweed body is back
in the news and your revenge complete,
painted day-glo orange and swung at the public
at sideshows in California. All thought you
straw, an ersatz fear to pay for
and therefore escape. You were shipped
between a thousand shows until your arm
came off in a carnie's grasp, revealing bones
My God, the thing is real

And the newspaper found you were an
old-time train robber from somewhere, Arkansas,
who at 50 won a bet that bullets
would take you before arrest
and after death you were exhibited
"as was the custom then" until
notoriety passed and you dried to
a wind toy for the weird Tarot gusts of today.

Was it really the wind that turned you in
as Billy the Kid asked *"Quien es?"*
Bonnie and Clyde took that drive
and the bullets came humming in
to punctuate your fame?

RENOVATING HELL

Even Hell must keep up with the times.
When the soul still knew its way
physical suffering sufficed.
But the levers, racks and furnaces broke down
eternal punishment left no time for maintenance.
The demons from Dante tired after centuries
of the stink of sinners in their own shit.
Beelzebub, for his part,
suffered from the symphony flies
always wove around him—
he began to refuse calls from
the cellular phones of the damned,
even felt compassion for clients
backstroking through the brimstone.

Now the lost soul finds bleak greeting rooms
burning with a cool, fluorescent light.
Hades and purgatory merged to cut costs.
Muzak plays songs the soul once loved
needled by strings and oversweet arrangements.

You always need one more
identity card or number and at every obstacle
transistorized greeting cards chirp
meaningless pledges of encouragement.
You will never get well, be processed,
leave this place. Or even learn
what you wait for.

Mephistopheles lounges outside the control room
where loop the automated tapes that echo down the halls.
Outside, in the sunlight,
the flies tumble and sing.
They too were fired by Hell's modernization plan.

THE CHILD MURDERER

The child murderer buys a newspaper
to see his latest work reviewed.
The coins he paid for the paper
radiate the warmth of his strong hand
as they lie in the register.
As he walks his new shoes creak slightly
like a sign swinging in the wind.

He is as careful with all details—
the gloves, the anonymous rope, the plastic bag—
as he is with his clothes.
He walks down the street with
a secret delight normal things magnify—
dog tethered to a parking meter,
the ferns outside the florist.
"Maybe," he thinks, "I'll send a
sympathy card 'From a Friend.' "

He, only he, can get away with it—
to charm and then chill without contradiction.
A man among men,
he reads the rest of the news on a park bench.
He adjusts the flower in his lapel.
Sparrows fly from the crumbs at his feet.
He smiles at a child, and stands.

PARLIAMENT ST. TABLEAU

A man is parked
on his back by the curb
in a suit torn and grey
arms legs weakly waving
like a rolled-over beetle.
One side of his face
raw red meat. The blood
draws eyes, wino hurt.

Two cops vertical pillars
who ignore normally his pain
look down blue arms folded
at his hands offering gestures
as if explaining himself.

THE SHUTTLE

Snow blows like white ash
across the net of windows
while Glenn Gould plays the Goldbergs again
his weaving fingers recalled from death
by shivering crystal
cutting through waves of frozen vinyl
he thought music better as
a symphony of splices and cuts
one grunt of his satisfaction
among a waterfall of notes
hands in the flurry of variation
like an epitaph

snow and Gould and Bach and the fireplace
consuming scraps of the wood
this house was built with last summer
the sun trapped in xylem and phloem
freed again to flower in golden heat

while I and the world watch again and again
a saturated blue sky the rocket enters
on a staff of smoke
to explode in a flaming corona
strangely beautiful
but seven lives blew out in that instant

of those seven all that's found at first
is one scorched glove on a beach
human hands always burnt when they approach
too closely the sun
and fall flaming long, whatever the wax

the astronauts are ash
now cloaked in the snow
blowing past the window's net
under which you lie in the fire's outer aura
the cat purring on your chest like a fat old sun
Gould stilled, the tone
arm switching back to rest

UNSCHEDULED TRAIN STOP

In the middle of
anywhere, against nightlit
ferns, we stop.

Beer stops,
sound breathes,
wind checks I.D.

Everything on the other
side of the mirror
stares back at us.

II. ARRIVALS & DEPARTURES LEVEL

"All passengers should arrive at least two hours before their plane leaves."

GROWING UP A BLOCK AWAY FROM JOHN McCRAE

Winter is withering through the dried grass
beside the river where you walked every day

November 13 and snow stays on the ground
your poem locked like a gear into the season

At John McCrae Public School we memorized your lines
and marched to this site Remembrance Day,

little boots in broken step, without the faintest idea
of what you meant: "we lived, felt dawn, saw sunset glow

loved and were loved. And now we lie in Flanders Fields"
where farmers still plow up bones from 1915.

Each year after the pumpkins grin and the first
snow stays, aging campaigners plant plastic poppies

like annual wounds on the chest of the public.
This is what your images become:

Parodies of the bloody blossoms over the graves
of farmers' sons gone to die for abstract ideas.

How far men will go to die. And now two Omega
wreaths stuffed with dried flowers flank

the bronze book where verdant and locked to time
your words march on . . . in Flanders Fields.

HALF-BAKED MOON

Hung in the absolutely heatless air
so clear every pock and crater shines
the full moon's a golf ball
waiting for the club of God to give it a thwack
or maybe it's just that my brain's
bent to that image ever since astronauts
teed off up there. The first low-g
drive straight down a grassless fairway.

We're too busy killing each other now,
and pretending we're not.
Who would bother to fire men
to the moon today? Or send a poet there,
instead of all those inarticulate
former fliers, physicists, jocks?

The best poems are still written
by those who've never been there, and the moon,
too cold for metaphor, exposes her injuries
to the irons of our inanity,
the woods of our stupidity,
the golf carts of our lunacy.

XMAS PAGEANT, 1961

At 13, I was the United Church's Joseph
my Mary a girl from College Avenue
so virginal that a blush
was new, disturbed her.
Our babe, a doll with oversized rubber head,
smelled like Eaton's.
Three wise men, resplendent in striped
bathrobes, towel turbans and
itchy cotton beards
brought gift-wrapped boxes of emptiness.
Frankincense was hard to find in Guelph,
myrrh too bitter for Ontario.

I thought Mary and I should at least
have a crush on each other
in Christmas spirit, when miracles,
births, warm animals and new stars
crowding the manger seemed sexy.
At 13, nearly everything did,
but she was as impossible to talk to
as a Japanese schoolgirl.
Only in the dumbshow of the pageant
could we touch, moist hands learning
the first step of high school courtship.

I had spent the Christmas before in Iraq
where the hills, bleached and biblical,
still bore sheep, shepherds wearing real robes,
goat songs fluted off the rocks.
Miracles were so long ago
they had worn to tracings on sun-blasted brick.
December was heat and sandstorms,

expensive stale goodies from the British import store
and chips and lemonade around the swimming pool
of the equally-British Alwiyah club.

Back in Guelph, I learned to step between worlds.
It was no stranger to play Joseph
with my white face and cracking voice
framed by snow sifting along the windows
than for Mary, with another exquisite blush,
to produce from my fertile imagining
a babe quiet and perfect enough
to attract teen-aged wise men
with their boxes of empty promise.

PAINTING OF "THE IMMACULATE CONCEPTION" IN THE SCOTTISH NATIONAL GALLERY

The virgin hovers in the air,
lofted by the jetstream
of life from her source.
Fat baby heads hang clustered
below her hem
and behind her more faces with steamy grins
condense from the clouds.

The virgin, to reassure herself,
recites again the angel's words:
One was the deal, and she then to be
honoured above all other women.
With hands steepled she prays,
and her eyes praise the light.

But the Lord's ways are manifold,
Like men, he can't stop at one
so he sows seed like dandelion down
through the air made fruitful
by the maiden's believing yes

Babies form and plop from her skirt
her halo a moon forever full
making her eggs quicken like a hen's.
Below, a saint on each side reacts.
The man spreads hands high in wonder and awe,
the woman clasps her robe tighter around.
No saint wants babies to perjure her penitence.
That poor, hovering girl will have enough.

DEAD SKUNK ON THE DON VALLEY PARKWAY

You smell, now, no worse
than the trucks rolling
on and around your blot of fur

Lanes leaf and merge everywhere
yet you made your way here, halfway
across, before something your bouquet

couldn't stop cancelled you.
You came, perhaps, to dance
among the white dashes and streaks

that define this black roadway
like hard-edge skunk art gone mad.
Maybe you had the time wrong:

a century ago, between wolf, fox and
hawk, you moved calmly here, your power held
under your tail's exclamation mark

Then, no one charged you at 100 per.
In skunk time you made sense.
Here, now, you catch only my eye

and I must drive on. But you cling
to me still, like the sweet inside your stink,
your midnight dance's grace.

HANGED MAN

To achieve sleep these nights
I require the pose
of the Hanged Man
one leg angled
and crossing the straight one
arms folded behind my head
then I wait for the dream
to hoist me by my foot
invert the world
and how I see it

from this point of view
the crowd's feet speak
heads hang from their necks
they watch me imagine and reconnect
the things that hang on me
here, my hair growing toward the earth
I am as much plant as man:
a mandrake, belladonna, weed
the blooms of evening comprehensible only to me
I used to think I was the Fool
about to walk off a cliff
now I need the suspension
the slow arc in the air

LACUNA

After Tim Buckley's high romantic melancholy
The needle circles in the null of his voice

wind knots and moans around the house
and about the throat of summer

and it's only August. On the sofa Miles
the cat makes a furred brown comma

exactly echoing the polished sea-shell
on the table. A black cat looks askance

from a poster on the wall, black plastic
crow hanging beside: a Ted Hughes toy.

Staccato drip from the kitchen tap counts
out the house's silence. Within the watch

of these witnesses we agree to become just friends
—no more rites of our bodies burning

and turning into light without end—
and your cheeks glisten with the change.

So warm and quiet here in your arms. Who
would think *we* would ever have

nothing to say. Our youth and partial truths
age into history like the cat, and these words.

LEAVING THE CAPE
(Cape Traverse, PEI)

Leaving the Cape
means pulling yourself out of a jigsaw
you were surprised you fit

Tiger lilies burning up the rain,
silver spider webs linking them,
herons musing in the stream that fills
and empties, empties and fills
as the shore bares and hides
its rippled sweep.

In honour of your departure,
a garland of kelp
garnished with mauve Irish moss
and set with immaculate shells spent
by the prodigal sea.

So load the car, lock the door,
take a last lungful of air
nourishing as broth,
then leave again
this living place that will stay
for you in closets and Kodachromes.
But this is only the human side.
The tides and clouds fill back in
this small gap in the puzzle
your leaving means.

ODE TO THE TD BANK
(On asking for my first small loan)

I have lived at the same address so long
that mail is slid through my mouth
and strangers grasp my hand to open
the door. Although I remain unmarried
all women work for me and offer up
their assets. The stars of the sky
I keep as jewels in my eye's vault.
I sleep in stocks and drink nothing
but bonded.

In fact limestone banks
chase me along the street trailing tapes
and begging for my magic valve kiss
to release the pressure of their
respectability. Most of all
I ask for money because I do not
even remotely need it, but only intend
to honour that minor art form
the won loan
which holds up all of Bay Street.

APPEARANCE IN PIER FOUR

This is me dining at Pier Four Restaurant
encompassed by lady tourists from Erie, PA
who find this city eerily
like their own, but bigger.
I regret lost loves.
The view is two-tone:
grey water streaked with silver,
a patched grey sky.
Why did I ever let her go?
When will I write another poem?
Where is my waiter?

Am I what I appear:
a white turtleneck bearing a beard,
writing nothing about the constitutional
crisis, but instead an unwilled song.
It's equally grey in Erie, PA.
The silver-coiffed widows near me
come from that close tone.
Her eyes were large, and I made them
angry, then sorry. One tourist says,
"You're a good sport. That much I'll say
for you. This scrod is out of this world."
So is where we are, sister,
Pier Four suspended by this poem
which arrives at last like a waiter.

The lake and sky merge monotones.
"Ladies," I long to yell
"Where did I go wrong? Should I marry?"
But another's discussing
her first husband, who was good for 30 years.

The people who now live only in my memory
move about restlessly. Did my grandfather
ever feel like this,
with his fine church-singing voice,
his cabinetry, his cancer?

EPITHALAMIUM FOR PAM

Two by two down through time
like branches splitting
to then divide into others
the women and men who made our blood
passed through this same gateway
of paper and lace, walked this aisle,
recited these words, ringed fingers
and kissed.

And we, who thought we might never wed,
are here, poised on time's fulcrum
in the Juniest, weddingest month of all
day of longest light
with a slim moon as new as that
solar gold around our heart's fingers
(but no train of white lace for you,
no old shoes and cans for our car).

This is really us, enacting the rite
naming the house we've built of each other
(because "husband" descends from "house-band"
true mate to house-wife)
Though we'll both cook and clean
and love and fight and wonder where
the money's going to come from
this is us, safe
in the edifice of our love.

In time we will join the earth
where in time roots will draw life
to send branches far above us
but we live here, we are now
wed, love.

ERIN'S BIRTH
The face of the earth was covered with water...
—The Book of Genesis

You waited until your due date
and in the honoured hour of the wolf
3:45, the first day of fall,
the start of Yom Kippur,
the closest approach of Mars to Earth,
the cusp of Libra and Virgo,
the waters that held you moved out.

We started you in Banff
cooking you up between sulphur springs and wine and
sliding skis through diamond fields of snow.
And we skated in the shade of Lake Louise's glacier,
balancing on thin steel over
the clear, crazed ice.
We made you with pleasure in the strength and softness
of our bodies, my tadpoles doing the Canadian crawl
to your mother's spore, the other half
of who you'd be.

You took root and held, your mother
sure from the start you'd stay.
She called me from a phone booth
to tell me she'd changed
into a song with accompaniment.
Then you hung on through her nausea and pain,
airplane flights, and a miserable month
of fighting Nova Scotia drizzle,
even through the rip spring made
as it wedged open winter's frozen grin.

You started to dance early:
at first a ball bouncing
to the red heartbeat above
then a tiny astronaut on a water walk
to the end of your line
so alert we called you Booter:
you'd kick every hand
or stethoscope laid on you
and so strong your motions
rippled your mother's belly.

Now surfing out on the muscular waves
you unbalance the world with your cry.

     —September 21-22, 1988

FOR ERIN

Small and new, you turn into me
as if you'd crawl inside where nothing hurts.

If I could open this man's body
I'd tuck you under my ribs
and warm you in the infra of my heart.
You whimper, awake, then instantly dream,
and forget the sharp things and cold lights and
hurts the world out here holds.

Forget the isolette that held you
a clear oven for your little loaf.
On your smile you slide back
to where you were always held
and cushioned and fed
and put your hands by your face again
the pose that made your birth take so long.

Maybe if you'd held them that way forever
you'd still be riding in the best ship there is
instead of this cold train
of emergency, test and therapy.
Crawl into me, small girl.
I'm holding my ribs up like an umbrella.

BACK TO YOU

On my fingers your scent
weaves a line through the day
back to you
Even the business letters I type
breathe a petalled smell
like perfume on the shoulder
of a three-piece suit.

What I learn of you
starts to thread parts of the world together
"your tiny hands are frozen" the aria
your grandfather, 90, still sang to you
and I find it again in the first book I read
after leaving you that day.

My sweat lines your sheets
and now you find companion bed
colder and quieter when
I'm not in it.
I know when you feel my absence
like I've known few things.
It's holding a rock in your hand long
enough that it's warm as blood.
Then you know as much as you can about
rock, about another.

PAM & NIMBUS

You and the cat
take this morning
to sleep the week off
she your purring grey pillow
you the mother she'll never become

suspended in the stillness at the height of summer
when heat tops its arc
before dropping through comet-coloured
autumn

nothing moves in the sky
bleached by the heat and water in the air
that wears away at us
swelling and carving our joints into driftwood

you and the cat, sleeping, form
a female unison
which I long to join
but I have a cup of coffee in one hand
a bottle of Windex in the other
then the cat stirs and gazes at me softly
no demand in her eye, only recognition
of the distance between us
so I put on the answering machine
and go to write my review
but this poem stretches out on the table
yawns and will not let me work
until I bury my face in its warm grey belly
float on summer, let it go

EXORCISM

I
Whenever I touch you too deeply it brings back again
the Latin lover from years ago.
This ghost's hand's stuck so deep in your heart
that he flips it away like a pizza
any time I get too close.

II
Worse, he doesn't even know he's haunting us.
His bodily form's balding in the Beaches,
going for boardwalks with his meal ticket
who you're glad to hear is heavy
around the thighs. These visitations from the living
are more difficult to clear.

III
Unreal though he is, his shadow
shrinks me again. Can I ever love you
as much as he hurt you? A difficult equation.
Our brains start weighing while dammit
he's back in our bed again
dividing us like an equal sign.

IV
Here's what we'll do, love: exorcise him.
He wanted to be a writer, so
I'll pen him in this pentacle of words
while you light three candles with your tears
incant his name over and over
until it's as void as any national brand's.

V
And when the glaze slides over his face
freezing him home, in front of the tube,
we'll trap him in a slot of dead time—
a car chase cut off, bullet suspended
in air like a hypnotized bee—
and though there'll always be that handprint
on your heart, our bed will hold only us.
No ghosts. A new start.

VARIATION ON A THEME BY ERIK SATIE

Delicately placed
spaces in between the notes
state the other melody:
the one not heard

Who says we only tune in
one channel at a time?

You do, silently.
You turn away, leave,
break it off

Between each gesture:
the ghost of you, happy to see me
face lit up by the lamp of me
and clothes flying off like leaves
from the lovely tree
underneath

In your stillness
I hear that other you singing
why, o why, o why
not?
Delicately placing me
in you
between the notes and
the nots

I'M IN LOVE WITH MY HOOVER

Today I declared my love at last
to my Hoover: plugged her in,
lay down beside her on the rug,
touched her power switch with my tongue
and let myself go in the sweet rush
of her indrawing air.

I love the way she empties
the dustfilled corners of my life.
She vanishes the rejection slips,
failed poems, duplicate bills
that fill my mail. I always take her
now when the doorbell rings.
A pimply boy selling chocolate bars
to benefit his school: I hoovered him up.
Another salesman, this time for his version
of the word of the Lord. Hoovered him too.
My whole family—hoovered! No more long
distance calls, Christmas gifts, guilt.
I hoovered off my moustache, then my whole face.
Sweet vacuum of anonymity.
Is she my real mother? I'll only know
when I hoover the rest of me
into the busy peace at the center
of her cyclone song.

DREAM GAME

They gave me four performers,
a square field divided into
four triangles, and a tent.
With these, I had to design
a ritual before my time was up.

I thought and thought, then
like Prospero, animated my kingdom.
One performer I dressed all in black
a shadow of someone not seen there.
She never spoke.
Across from her was another
shimmering in silver Mylar
so all you saw was the world around her,
never the person inside.
One of the males was the speaker,
pacing his commentary to the cadence of his steps.
The last one sang wordlessly,
a soaring line of melody,
but stopped sometimes
to illuminate a detail with the laser in his hand.

They paced in step along the sides
of their separate triangles,
then met at the center and somehow
changed. Above them, the tent,
suspended in air, freed at last of pegs,
rippled in the wind like light
flowing across Mylar,
draining into darkness.

ALL THAT COUNTS

I make the same left turn every day
a small orbit on the advance green
I followed tight behind the car ahead
and flicked my eyes to the left

20 feet away, a Mustang headed straight for me,
brakes locked, the woman at the wheel
staring at me with the craven apology
fatal errors inspire

she smoked by my rear bumper with a foot to spare
and went right through the intersection
her tires still singing

so I lived to teach my classes,
go home to my daughter's laughter,
write this poem

the luck that for 40 years
has kept my bones unbroken
and saved me when my own sense failed
rode with me once more

but luck is a human imagining:
an accident of physics saved me—
like the whiffle of wind that directs
a bullet into the shoulder instead of heart
or the grand piano falling from the hoist
that goes fortissimo a stride behind your shoe—

and my own impatience saved me too. A second slower
making the turn, and I'd be the sticker
on her car's bumper, her craven apologies
would be to my family.

The cliché is true. The grass seems to shine,
and when I drive home tonight, carefully,
I'll give my wife and daughter the hug
that affirms we're all still here.
Lucky to be here,
lucky
to be.

CAT ENDING
(in memory of Zach)

you never asked much:
shyly slipping in our door one day
a small cloud of grey
extra front toes your gift

when I was sick
you lay in bed with me and dispensed
healing purrs
when my wife went into labour
you laid one grey paw on her
belly and kept vigil
for our baby
and then you played pillow and toy
and best friend for her

when the death virus slid into your veins
like a vicious stray along a moonless fence
you stayed yourself until you were ready
and then you simply stopped
eating, drinking, playing

you knew it was time to go to your next house
so you curled up in a basement box
asking nothing, protesting not at all
you died with your eyes open

I hope I can meet my own death
with the acceptance and release
you gave us

THE MAN ON OUR PORCH

rang all the doorbells
and when we answered
he was eating the dirt from the big planter pot
and throwing it around.
Skinny, no teeth, dark eyes that looked
right through us into a much scarier world.

So Hugh and I held him
while he thrashed around, kicked
the glass door with his work boots.
His only jewelery was a hospital ID band.
Through his grunts and wails we could make out
just two messages: "Afraid!" and "Kill me!"

We tried to calm him, hold his hands, while we waited
the forever it took help to come.
Sometimes he seemed to see us, knew we weren't foes,
but then the brick wall he lunged at would melt
and demons only he saw came through.
Although he fought, he wasn't trying to hurt us, just it
(and who wrote "the dog bites itself
to hurt the pain"?)
Then he tried to throw himself off the railing
choked on the dirt in his throat when I gave him water
When the police came to take him,
he grabbed a young one's baton
and was instantly kicked for his trouble.
The kindly older cop told us
the man was MI, "Mentally incompetent."
And he'd talk to the young cop,
realized we might think their actions were not
"appropriate" but "we gotta deal with what they do.
If we perceive a threat...."

The man who perceived threat everywhere
was thrown back into the official stream
of test, assessment, mandatory supervision.
"Schizophrenic," I thought, "means split skull."
I could almost see the axe between his hemispheres,
handle ready for anything to jerk it
as I swept the dirt off the porch,
tried to tell my daughter
what "crazy" really meant.

PROPOSAL FOR PRINCE CHARLES

You were born to the richer house
of Windsor, while I inherited nothing
and have earned every title I own
but I always felt some ties to you:
we were born about the same time.
Both married and had children late
and laughed at Monty Python (although
I probably liked their Prince Charles
routine more than you did).

Prince, the time has come
to trade lives. You've messed up.
Mom will never retire now;
your thin charm has worn off
even for your subjects
and I'm tired of poverty, driving 11-year-old econoboxes,
paying for daycare.

So here's the deal:
I get the Aston Martins, the Jags,
the Scottish estates, the annual income.
In return I promise to shake hands warmly
with all, include them in a brief chat
that never touches politics. I'll make no sex calls
on my cellular phones, and will remain civil to Diana
although she's not really my type either.
And you get the six courses per term to teach—
a real job at last!—the bills, the basement apartment,
the garden of rust on the '83 Acadian.

The experience will benefit us both:
you can write a book called
Prince Among the Commoners. Just before our

deaths, around the age of 85, we'll switch back.
I can't stand state funerals or the damp
floor of Westminster Abbey.
You can go out the royal way,
and I'll have my remaining friends
read a few poems, get drunk,
roast marshmallows on the fire of me
and feed my ashes to the lilacs.
We'll both learn something, Prince,
so here's my keys, my mail, my life.
I'll be at the Palace gates tomorrow
to collect my Princehood from you.

BEING IN/SEEING THE BODY

When I was 30, the poet I loved
wrote about me: "your body
beautiful as a young boy's"

I was never your standard-issue tall Adonis
but felt smug in my well-proportioned shortness
my good ex-bike-racer's legs
my strong chest, big hands.

Tomorrow I'm 45
and the mirror shows me
a posthumous work by Antonio Gaudi
a cautionary gargoyle to adorn
the melting cathedral of Barcelona
everything's still there
but softening and easing southward
like a candle figure
lit just a little too long
in my mind, I still move with power and grace
I took for granted at 30
but my body now inhabits the middle kingdom
where nothing can be taken for granted
surreal little pains with no apparent cause
light up my knees and shoulder
like smuggled fireworks let off in daytime
long after the allocated holiday.
I still look not too bad
in a line-up with my peers
the beer-belly's of modest scope
my waist only up to 33
my weight around 150
hair still curly and brown
but dimples and wrinkles are evenly matched
lines written for good on my face

from almost half a century of construing
how time draws us ever on
despite all the artifices of memory and denial
and poetry itself.
Time now teaches us how to become the stranger
we never would have recognized when a child.

OPEN HOUSE

This must be his gift for the bride:
passion so untrammeled that he still
shouts and writhes
although three men sit on him
unable either to hurt him—
circling, silent onlookers record every move—
or to let the handle
of his emotional grenade release.

I can barely see him under the men on him.
My daughter, holding my hand, is puzzled—
this must be some new adult game.
She is fresh from riding tired ponies
at the other side of the quad, and
here are men riding a man.

Torn turf supports them, and the leaden sky
presses down like a printmaking plate.
The bride is invisible
but ritual accessories surround this knot
of one man's rage:
white stretch limo at the college's curb
with crepe streamers and paper flowers,
mute hangers-on in Syd Silver tuxes,
photographer hung with lenses, batteries, cords.

The police lead him away,
his performance complete,
He gave the bride her only present
unmediated by questions of taste or cost:
would her new husband have roared or
ripped the ground for her?
Would I?

Whether he is the jilted boyfriend
or madman whose comet's orbit
intersected this event by accident:
he had intensity of feeling she
will long for. She will keep this memory
when the wedding albums stay closed:
he loved her enough to do this

I long for emotion
only bruises and handcuffs can frame;
but my daughter's small hand
keeps my balloon on the ground
so I save this moment for reference
when suitors call on her.

STROKE/OBLIQUE
(for my mother)

An errant line stopped its flow
to your left brain
like an oblique/ cancelling a name
a little cerebral-vascular accident
caused by a fragment of arterial plaque
loose in the sanguine tide
that ebbs and whispers along the organ pipes
and flourishes of the body

now in half your brain nothing may move
but snow, falling in endless hush

Seeing you in the hospital at 2:30 a.m.
I thought you might die
but day by day you put more back together
than anyone thought you could
first you know your children's faces
but not our names
then with your manners as proper as ever
delicately hold the spoon upside down and try
to balance bland hospital morsels on its bowl
when handed your toothpaste you gravely
consult the mirror and spread
Crest neatly around your lips
At 73 you relearn the simple things of life
while in the left half of your brain
nothing moves but snow sliding down

Asked to write your name you carefully letter out
"QUART"
you who took on the *Globe's* Friday cross-word every week
"gyre" "schist" and "owlet" (Hamlet's night bird?) familiar
as the irises in your gardens

which you still admire but can't say the name for
Those nights we sat by the fire around a card table
and played Scrabble where words count triple
now few words come out the way you will
although you know what you want to say
snow slips between the syllables
and your intelligence can't find the way out
from your eyes the same smart little girl
whose family couldn't understand
looks out to see if I understand
you see mirrored in my eyes the snow again
that obliques your meaning

At first you are reduced to the elements
of a nod, a smile, a hand's assent
you regain language like an earthquake survivor
rebuilding her house, stone by stone

One image of you
my brain will hold until it stills
you doze in a chair near the cabin
shaded from the late August sun,
the same place where your dying daughter
sat ten years ago
and the loss and grief leave your face
revealing its strength and gentleness
comfortable in your bones, among the carolling birds
you once knew by name
you sit
safe in a word
bigger than any my brain knows

III. TWISTING THE TONGUE

"Hello? Is this the occupant? I'm making a telephone poll—could you tell me to whom you are listening on your telephone at this very moment?"

—Walt Kelly, *Equal Time for Pogo*

CANADIAN LOVE SONG

INSTRUCTIONS: read this out loud either A) nude in a forest during the summer or B) while a friend hums as high as possible and occasionally slaps your body.

I have an itch
which is you
calamine pink
mosquito blue

Floating I smell
your tender skin
the blood you bubble
to draw me in

I've got an itch
that wants your bite
in humming sun
in hatching night

Your touch sings
"Sting me awake
Scratch away these
weeks without wings"

In tent, in bag
portaging canoe
mosquito pink
calamine blue

THE PERCEIVABILITY OF POETRY

'*The Native Hollander wears wooden shoes.*'
'*Nebraska has no seacoast.*'
'*The daisy is a common wildflower.*'
    As these syllables, words and sentences come in over the telephones, stand-ins for millions of Bell System subscribers rate them for clarity of reception.
                      —Bell Tel ad in 1959 *Scientific American*

True, few will listen when poetry calls:
they think they've got the wrong line
a harangue in some exotic tongue
a satellite call from Mars
a subscription offer to eternity

but I'm here to tell you
Nebraska has no sequels
the daisy has come in wildfire
Nate, in collander wears, wouldn't choose

and this news has the clarity of any you receive
poetry's in the curve from mouth to ear
even as we talk we agitate carbon grains
that squeeze our words into a spiral cord
and boil them out the other end
and you still say poetry isn't clear.
Well, the word is a wildly common weed
but I seek no hose nor will Ned ask her
and the days you see are wood
shooting onto a seacoast

what has more clarity than a daisy?
And yet I mean by "daisy": time, change,
pollen on the flying legs of bees
the sun surrounded by our white faces
the shaded meaning of any word

the petals that burst from the ear
when I sing

now tell me what you heard in what I said
and I'll let you go

THE WHITE PAGE
(in memory of bp nichol)

Facing the white page.
Its feature: featurelessness.
Make the first mark, start, invoke a chain
that pulls down the curtain on the other chains.
The page, white
Arctic expanse, space gone crazy. Go
crazy, pee your name
in drifting loops across the page,
calligraph it with a brush dipped in gas,
sign it with a match. The burning page
frozen.

Erase. Delete. Reverse.
The page still white. White always. Waiting.
Nose to the page, you feel distant movement,
molecules chanting along the lines, rhythm.
A tiny black dot in the white distance.
All words condensed into one whole.
The dot growing, racing at you.
Doppler effect of sidebands, parallel text,
sliding tones pulled along in the slipstream.
The whole page, black, bursting around you.
Roar in your ears of many languages, multiple
lines. Black shreds of punctuation eclipse, fall away.
The page white again, but now a negative.
From memory you begin to fill the page, alter it.
Telling the page, lining its altar with
your symbols finally aligned,
the cup, the cloth, speaking lips.
The blood-red wine alters the memory.
You were never Catholic.
Is the page now someone else's? Strike out. Crumple.
A match to it. Reflecting: this white page.

Writing as the shadow, adumbration, not too much light
on the subject. Leave room for language
to uncoil in the shade.
Page, bring me my helmet and sword.
Is it false to take meaning from the sound?
Aren't all things signs?
Slaying the page with a single stroke.
Writer's dream on white sheets of night
and coming back to dance on the page
next morning. Feet brush by like vowels
along the lip of the page. The center, still white,
the heart of the page. Untouched, unlined.
Acquiescent, questioning. Mute, demanding.
A state that mind never achieves
it's so lined with words with music,
with hunger for the white page.

RIMBAUD DELIBERATELY MISTRANSLATED (I)

A habitant horse, his indigo Detroit boulevardier
with sable seats smoking
like a broom rode down the distraught band
June's crystals in the continent
the boys punting in the woods.
As the tavern has the roue,
the devil's dogs half bark.
Sinister fair, no ire is in I
Nor the nap at last of the porters,
the posters in loom
lotion fumes as the ant pisses
In the foaming ocean
Rich city, retch softly your almond fruit
Vile Bat! Tile!

RIMBAUD DELIBERATELY MISTRANSLATED (II)

A souffle operates on the breeches of the cloisters
where the rouged tarts pivot in the fog
and disperse the limits of fire,
clipping the crosses of arms

I long for a vignette, metal Apu, yeah!
though he sweats dice and dew with caresses
a vexed glass indicates the assay;
bombed bread trucks and contorted sophists
simmered in a soup of raves and billiard balls

the Italian sun
insolently gazes at our nursery
Grandfather Highway stares back at him
between them a glaze forms of blemished law
like a breast filling the moon

the souffle goes icy, arrested, in orange
Sodom caught in salt, stilling the ferocious arms of beds
while the postman delivers a monkey
found fucking in Suffolk
the pet of a worn sorcerer there

O clapping pots, aunts and dogs
the souffle disperses the limits of faith

RIMBAUD DELIBERATELY MISTRANSLATED (III)

The grace of Phil's pain!
The author of front tones can run
flowers in the bays, days you preciously
bowl, REM's you ain't.
Touché to the bruin, your juice crews.
They crack lissomely. To your boy dream
reassembling a zither, you tantamount to a circle,
Dan in a blonde bra. The tone of the court's bat,
Dan serving his doubt a double sex.
Promising toilet, L.A. night, movie does mention to
set quiche, set second of quiche, eat jam
(DeGaulle's).

WILLIAM TELL'S SON SPEAKS

I do wish Dad
would give up on this:
but he stands there still, too far away,
one eye pulled into a paternal squint
sighting along that damned shaft
while I wait, absurd, still life
with an apple in my hair.

At this point in my storybooks
someone always gallops to the rescue
maybe it'll be the Lone Ranger
riding on the wave of his overture
to point out with his Colt .45
how my father might reconsider
this practice of targeting me.
But no hooves arrive.

"Have faith," Father tells me,
"I never miss."
"Miss once, and I'll be never,"
I mutter, but he doesn't hear,
one ear tuned to his Swiss watchmaker God,
the other to the wavering wind.

So I'm Isaac and he's willing to bet me
on one more test of his belief
Or he's Isaac Newton, set to kill
The apple of gravity with the arrow
of his thought. Me, I'm just a body at rest.

What does he need me for?
He could skewer this fruit on a fence post
with just as fine a shot. A post that would also
look better wearing a miss

than, my smooth boy's brow would.
But it's too late to tell him anything.
His fingers are just releasing the string,
while his lips hiss: "This is for you,
son!"

HAGAR THE HALFLING
(for the ladies)

See Hagar the Halfling rule hyperspace
cutting a swath through the ladies
with his virtual pen-is-
greater than sword
coming onto them all MUSH-y and MOO-y
offering virtual pleasures obtainable
only from his electronic node of
the golden-grained Prairies

and he's intelligent, respectable, creative, wise
taking everyone in with his rehearsed caring voice
collecting pix to choose the next victim

but when the screen goes dead and
the cloaking mechanism fails, underneath
he's the same old story (pitiful,
if he hadn't hurt so many)
the white-belted cocktail-lounging shark
wedding ring hidden in an inside pocket
"the wife don't understand me" speech
ready for back-up, the ultimate offer
"I'll leave her for you soon" still warm
from a lying laser printer
offering anything to get textual sex
from the ladies who still have faith
they'll find a heart large enough to pulse
in non-electronic time with their own
at last Hagar the Halfling
retreats, leaving burned hearths and hearts,
back home to do battle with the demons
his conjuring fingers hid from all
who knew him only in electronic space.

THE WORLD SCREENED

The world through your window
is screened into rows of tiny cubes

that mean we can remake
the world by shifting them

a pure pane of sky
shines from the pine's arthritic roots

the library is strewn along the walk
which itself winds over

branches, bedrooms. Shadows of things start
elsewhere and cross where they might be cloud

The pedestrian's two left eyes
regard the sun strolling on her leash

as they move cube by cube over the clear blue lawn
her heart is (not is like) a bird.

About John Oughton

John Oughton was born in Guelph, Ontario, and spent his formative years there, except for two years in Egypt and Iraq. He has since lived in Japan and Nova Scotia as well as Toronto. Oughton studied literature at York University in Toronto, and the Naropa Institute in Boulder, Colorado, where he worked closely with Allen Ginsberg, Anne Waldman, and Robert Duncan.

Active as a literary journalist and reviewer, he has published three previous books of poetry: *Taking Tree Trains* (1973); *Gearing of Love* (1984); *Mata Hari's Lost Words* (1988). A contributor to literary groups on the Internet for the last decade, he is one of the first members of the active creative writing list, CREWRT-L. His poetry and photography have appeared in several anthologies and on Web pages and periodicals throughout North America. Currently, he is completing a doctorate in education at the Ontario Institute for Studies in Education, teaching at a community college, and free-lancing as a writer and computer consultant.

Pecan Grove Press Titles in Print

A Time to Be Born
    by Olga Samples Davis
Somewhere Between Hither and Yearn
    by Ritalinda D'Andrea
Dragonfly
    by Vince Gotera
A Measured Response
    edited by H. Palmer Hall
Snow in South Texas
    by Cynthia Harper
A Certain Attitude
    edited by Laura Kennelly
Choc'lit Milk and Whiskey Voices
    by Jo LeCoeur
Pointed Home: A Cross-Country Essay
    by W. Scott Olsen
At the Border: Winter Lights
    by Carol Coffee Reposa
Out of Nowhere, the Body's Shape
    by Beth Simon
Stone Garden
    by Barbara Stanush
The Skies Here
    by Rachel Barenblat
Counting Out the Millennium
    by John Oughton

and forthcoming from Pecan Grove Press:
    East of Omaha
        by Edward Byrne